I0140317

MY BOOK OF THANKS

ISBN:978-3-9503878-4-1

(serendii)

Day 1

What are
you thankful
for today?

Day 2

Thank You!

Day 3

What are
you thankful
for today?

Day 4

Thank You!

Day 5

What are
you thankful
for today?

Day 6

Thank You!

Day 7

What are
you thankful
for today?

Day 8

Thank You!

Day 9

What are
you thankful
for today?

Day 10

Thank You!

Day 11

What are
you thankful
for today?

Day 12

Day 13

What are
you thankful
for today?

Day 14

Thank You!

Day 15

What are
you thankful
for today?

Day 16

Thank You!

Day 17

What are
you thankful
for today?

Day 18

Thank You!

Day 19

What are
you thankful
for today?

Day 20

Thank You!

Day 21

What are
you thankful
for today?

Day 22

Thank You!

Day 23

What are
you thankful
for today?

Day 24

Thank You!

Day 25

What are
you thankful
for today?

Day 26

Thank You!

Day 27

What are
you thankful
for today?

Day 28

Thank You!

Day 29

What are
you thankful
for today?

Day 30

Thank You!

Day 31

What are
you thankful
for today?

Day 32

Day 33

What are
you thankful
for today?

Day 34

Thank You!

Day 35

Day 36

Thank You!

Day 37

What are
you thankful
for today?

Day 38

Thank You!

Day 39

What are
you thankful
for today?

Day 40

Thank You!

Day 41

What are
you thankful
for today?

Day 42

Thank You!

Day 43

What are
you thankful
for today?

Day 44

Thank You!

Day 45

What are
you thankful
for today?

Day 46

Thank You!

Day 47

Day 48

Thank You!

Day 49

What are
you thankful
for today?

Day 50

Thank You!

Day 51

What are
you thankful
for today?

Day 52

Thank You!

Day 53

What are
you thankful
for today?

Day 54

Thank You!

Day 55

What are
you thankful
for today?

Day 56

Thank You!

Day 57

What are
you thankful
for today?

Day 58

Thank You!

Day 59

What are
you thankful
for today?

Day 60

Thank You!

Day 61

Day 62

Thank You!

Day 63

What are
you thankful
for today?

Day 64

Thank You!

Day 65

What are
you thankful
for today?

Day 66

Day 67

What are
you thankful
for today?

Day 68

Thank You!

Day 69

What are
you thankful
for today?

Day 70

Thank You!

Day 71

What are
you thankful
for today?

Day 72

Thank You!

Day 73

What are
you thankful
for today?

Day 74

Thank You!

Day 75

What are
you thankful
for today?

Day 76

Thank You!

Day 77

What are
you thankful
for today?

Day 78

Thank You!

Day 79

What are
you thankful
for today?

Day 80

Thank You!

Day 81

What are
you thankful
for today?

Day 82

Thank You!

Day 83

What are
you thankful
for today?

Day 84

Thank You!

Day 85

What are
you thankful
for today?

Day 86

Thank You!

Day 87

What are
you thankful
for today?

Day 88

Thank You!

Day 89

What are
you thankful
for today?

Day 90

Thank You!

Day 91

What are
you thankful
for today?

Day 92

Thank You!

Day 93

Day 94

Thank You!

Day 95

Day 96

Thank You!

Day 97

Day 98

Thank You!

Day 99

What are
you thankful
for today?

Day 100

Thank You!

Day 101

What are
you thankful
for today?

Day 102

Thank You!

Day 103

What are
you thankful
for today?

Day 104

Thank You!

Day 105

What are
you thankful
for today?

Day 106

Thank You!

Day 107

Day 108

Thank You!

Day 109

Day 110

Thank You!

Day 111

What are
you thankful
for today?

Day 112

Thank You!

Day 113

What are
you thankful
for today?

Day 114

Thank You!

Day 115

What are
you thankful
for today?

Day 116

Day 117

What are
you thankful
for today?

Day 118

Thank You!

Day 119

What are
you thankful
for today?

Day 120

Thank You!

Day 121

What are
you thankful
for today?

Day 122

Thank You!

Day 123

Day 124

Thank You!

Day 125

What are
you thankful
for today?

Day 126

Thank You!

Day 127

What are
you thankful
for today?

Day 128

Thank You!

Day 129

What are
you thankful
for today?

Day 130

Thank You!

Day 131

What are
you thankful
for today?

Day 132

Thank You!

Day 133

What are
you thankful
for today?

Day 134

Thank You!

Day 135

What are
you thankful
for today?

Day 136

Thank You!

Day 137

What are
you thankful
for today?

Day 138

Thank You!

Day 139

What are
you thankful
for today?

Day 140

Thank You!

Day 141

What are
you thankful
for today?

Day 142

Thank You!

Day 143

What are
you thankful
for today?

Day 144

Thank You!

Day 145

What are
you thankful
for today?

Day 146

Thank You!

Day 147

What are
you thankful
for today?

Day 148

Thank You!

Day 149

Day 150

Day 151

What are
you thankful
for today?

Day 152

Thank You!

Day 153

What are
you thankful
for today?

Day 154

Thank You!

Day 155

What are
you thankful
for today?

Day 156

Thank You!

Day 157

What are
you thankful
for today?

Day 158

Thank You!

Day 159

What are
you thankful
for today?

Day 160

Thank You!

Day 161

What are
you thankful
for today?

Day 162

Thank You!

Day 163

What are
you thankful
for today?

Day 164

Day 165

What are
you thankful
for today?

Day 166

Thank You!

Day 167

What are
you thankful
for today?

Day 168

Thank You!

Day 169

What are
you thankful
for today?

Day 170

Thank You!

Day 171

What are
you thankful
for today?

Day 172

Thank You!

Day 173

Day 174

Thank You!

Day 175

What are
you thankful
for today?

Day 176

Thank You!

Day 177

Day 178

Thank You!

Day 179

What are
you thankful
for today?

Day 180

Thank You!

Day 181

What are
you thankful
for today?

Day 182

Thank You!

Day 183

What are
you thankful
for today?

Day 184.

Thank You!

Day 185

What are
you thankful
for today?

Day 186

Day 187

What are
you thankful
for today?

Day 188

Thank You!

Day 189

What are
you thankful
for today?

Day 190

Thank You!

Day 191

What are
you thankful
for today?

Day 192

Thank You!

Day 193

What are
you thankful
for today?

Day 194

Day 195

What are
you thankful
for today?

Day 196

Thank You!

Day 197

What are
you thankful
for today?

Day 198

Thank You!

Day 199

What are
you thankful
for today?

Day 200

Thank You!

Day 201

Day 202

Thank You!

Day 203

Day 204

Thank You!

Day 205

What are
you thankful
for today?

Day 206

Thank You!

Day 207

Day 208

Thank You!

Day 209

What are
you thankful
for today?

Day 210

Thank You!

Day 211

Day 212

Thank You!

Day 213

What are
you thankful
for today?

Day 214

Thank You!

Day 215

What are
you thankful
for today?

Day 216

Thank You!

Day 217

What are
you thankful
for today?

Day 218

Thank You!

Day 219

Day 220

Thank You!

Day 221

What are
you thankful
for today?

Day 222

Thank You!

Day 223

What are
you thankful
for today?

Day 224

Thank You!

Day 225

What are
you thankful
for today?

Day 226

Thank You!

Day 227

What are
you thankful
for today?

Day 228

Thank You!

Day 229

What are
you thankful
for today?

Day 230

Thank You!

Day 231

What are
you thankful
for today?

Day 232

Thank You!

Day 233

What are
you thankful
for today?

Day 234

Thank You!

Day 235

What are
you thankful
for today?

Day 236

Thank You!

Day 237

What are
you thankful
for today?

Day 238

Thank You!

Day 239

Day 240

Thank You!

Day 241

What are
you thankful
for today?

Day 242

Thank You!

Day 243

What are
you thankful
for today?

Day 244

Day 245

What are
you thankful
for today?

Day 246

Day 247

What are
you thankful
for today?

Day 248

Thank You!

Day 249

What are
you thankful
for today?

Day 250

Thank You!

Day 251

Day 252

Thank You!

Day 253

What are
you thankful
for today?

Day 254

Thank You!

Day 255

What are
you thankful
for today?

Day 256

Thank You!

Day 257

What are
you thankful
for today?

Day 258

Thank You!

Day 259

What are
you thankful
for today?

Day 260

Thank You!

Day 261

Day 262

Thank You!

Day 263

What are
you thankful
for today?

Day 264

Thank You!

Day 265

What are
you thankful
for today?

Day 266

Thank You!

Day 267

What are
you thankful
for today?

Day 268

Thank You!

Day 269

What are
you thankful
for today?

Day 270

Thank You!

Day 271

What are
you thankful
for today?

Day 272

Thank You!

Day 273

Day 274

Thank You!

Day 275

Day 276

Thank You!

Day 277

What are
you thankful
for today?

Day 278

Thank You!

Day 279

Day 280

Thank You!

Day 281

What are
you thankful
for today?

Day 282

Thank You!

Day 283

What are
you thankful
for today?

Day 284

Thank You!

Day 285

What are
you thankful
for today?

Day 286

Thank You!

Day 287

What are
you thankful
for today?

Day 288

Thank You!

Day 289

What are
you thankful
for today?

Day 290

Thank You!

Day 291

What are
you thankful
for today?

Day 292

Thank You!

Day 293

Day 294

Thank You!

Day 295

What are
you thankful
for today?

Day 296

Thank You!

Day 297

What are
you thankful
for today?

Day 298

Thank You!

Day 299

What are
you thankful
for today?

Day 300

Thank You!

Day 301

Day 302

Thank You!

Day 303

What are
you thankful
for today?

Day 304

Thank You!

Day 305

What are
you thankful
for today?

Day 306

Thank You!

Day 307

What are
you thankful
for today?

Day 308

Thank You!

Day 309

What are
you thankful
for today?

Day 310

Thank You!

Day 311

What are
you thankful
for today?

Day 312

Thank You!

Day 313

What are
you thankful
for today?

Day 314

Thank You!

Day 315

What are
you thankful
for today?

Day 316

Thank You!

Day 317

What are
you thankful
for today?

Day 318

Day 319

What are
you thankful
for today?

Day 320

Thank You!

Day 321

What are
you thankful
for today?

Day 322

Thank You!

Day 323

What are
you thankful
for today?

Day 324

Thank You!

Day 325

What are
you thankful
for today?

Day 326

Thank You!

Day 327

What are
you thankful
for today?

Day 328

Thank You!

Day 329

What are
you thankful
for today?

Day 330

Thank You!

Day 331

What are
you thankful
for today?

Day 332

Thank You!

Day 333

What are
you thankful
for today?

Day 334

Thank You!

Day 335

What are
you thankful
for today?

Day 336

Day 337

What are
you thankful
for today?

Day 338

Thank You!

Day 339

What are
you thankful
for today?

Day 340

Thank You!

Day 341

What are
you thankful
for today?

Day 342

Thank You!

Day 343

What are
you thankful
for today?

Day 344

Thank You!

Day 345

What are
you thankful
for today?

Day 346

Thank You!

Day 347

What are
you thankful
for today?

Day 348

Thank You!

Day 349

What are
you thankful
for today?

Day 350

Thank You!

Day 351

What are
you thankful
for today?

Day 352

Thank You!

Day 353

What are
you thankful
for today?

Day 354

Thank You!

Day 355

Day 356

Thank You!

Day 357

What are
you thankful
for today?

Day 358

Thank You!

Day 359

What are
you thankful
for today?

Day 360

Thank You!

Day 361

What are
you thankful
for today?

Day 362

Thank You!

Day 363

What are
you thankful
for today?

Day 364

Thank You!

Day 365

What are
you thankful
for today?

www.ingramcontent.com/pod-product-compliance
Lightning Source LLC
Chambersburg PA
CBHW070012110426
42741CB00034B/1197